being a dj

Lisa Regan and
Matt Anniss

First published in 2015 by Wayland

Copyright © Wayland 2015

Dewey Number: 793.3'1954-dc22
ISBN: 978 0 7502 9442 3
Library ebook ISBN: 978 0 7502 7394 7

0 9 8 7 6 5 4 3 2 1

Concept by Joyce Bentley

Commissioned by Debbie Foy and
Rasha Elsaeed

Produced for Wayland by Calcium
Designer: Paul Myerscough
Editor: Sarah Eason

MIX
Paper from
responsible sources
FSC® C104740
FSC
www.fsc.org

Wayland is an imprint of
Hachette Children's Group
Part of Hodder & Stoughton
Carmelite House
50 Victoria Embankment
London EC4Y 0DZ

An Hachette UK Company
www.hachette.co.uk

www.hachettechildrens.co.uk

Printed in China

Acknowledgements: Alamy: Andrew Aitchison 21,
Lebrecht Music and Arts Photo Library 22–23;
Dreamstime: Dmytro Konstantynov 1; Getty:
WireImage 8; iStock: Jan Otto 17tl, 29t;
Shutterstock: 26kot 31tr, Akva 6–7, Anatema
4–5, Anky 24b, Yuri Arcurs 30l, Ayakovlev.com
28b, Maxim Blinkov 28t, Corepics cover, 30b,
Bairachnyi Dmitry 3br, Dwphotos 2b, 26–27,
Hurricane 25, Joyfull 14, 15, Fedor Kondratenko
28c, Kzenon 17tr, Winston Link 31b, Nikkytok 2–3,
Olly 29br, Vitechek2 10; Sara Simms 2tl, 12; Tom
Thorpe 2tr, 16–17, 17tc; Wikipedia: Bigtimepeace
2c, 20, Stu Spivack 18–19, Jay Want 19.

thepeople

thegear

thetalk

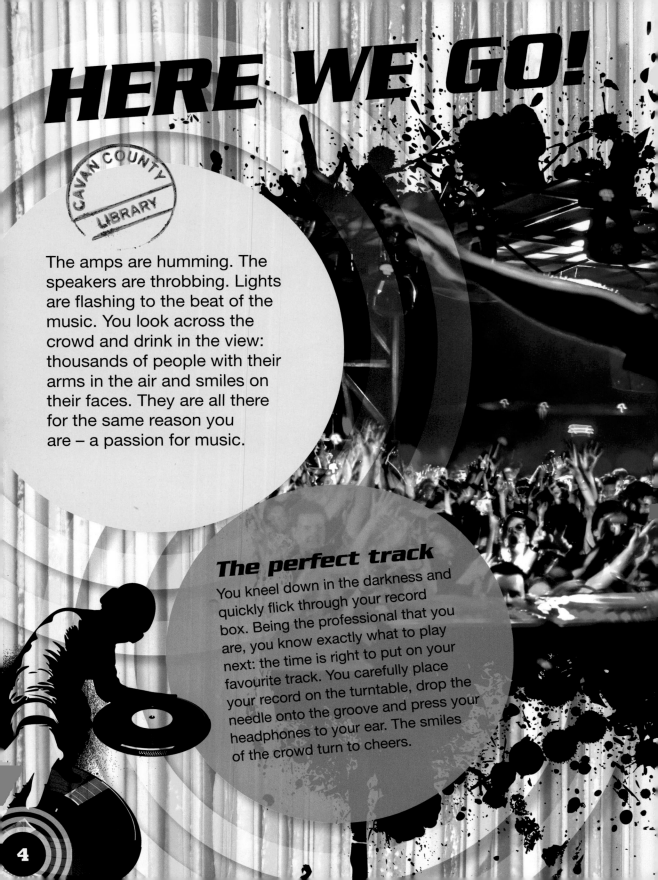

HERE WE GO!

The amps are humming. The speakers are throbbing. Lights are flashing to the beat of the music. You look across the crowd and drink in the view: thousands of people with their arms in the air and smiles on their faces. They are all there for the same reason you are – a passion for music.

The perfect track

You kneel down in the darkness and quickly flick through your record box. Being the professional that you are, you know exactly what to play next: the time is right to put on your favourite track. You carefully place your record on the turntable, drop the needle onto the groove and press your headphones to your ear. The smiles of the crowd turn to cheers.

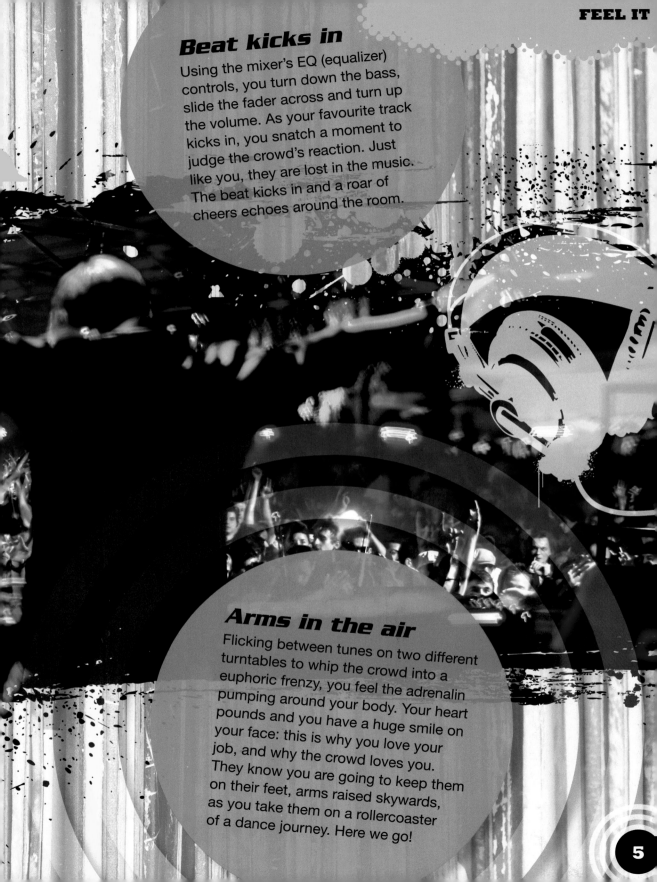

Beat kicks in

Using the mixer's EQ (equalizer) controls, you turn down the bass, slide the fader across and turn up the volume. As your favourite track kicks in, you snatch a moment to judge the crowd's reaction. Just like you, they are lost in the music. The beat kicks in and a roar of cheers echoes around the room.

Arms in the air

Flicking between tunes on two different turntables to whip the crowd into a euphoric frenzy, you feel the adrenalin pumping around your body. Your heart pounds and you have a huge smile on your face: this is why you love your job, and why the crowd loves you. They know you are going to keep them on their feet, arms raised skywards, as you take them on a rollercoaster of a dance journey. Here we go!

HEY, MR' DJ!

Take one person and put him or her in charge of playing music for an audience, and what do you get? A disc jockey – known to the world as a DJ.

Clubbing it

Most DJs play music that people can dance to. They entertain crowds at private parties, music festivals and in nightclubs. DJs are passionate about music and know which songs work well as a set – a carefully chosen selection of tracks guaranteed to fill a dance floor. Using a range of mixing skills and some simple equipment, DJs must choose and mix the best music to keep the crowd on its feet.

Scratch that itch

Some DJs use special turntable tricks such as scratching and beat juggling. These DJs are known as turntablists – so called because they use turntables, vinyl records and a mixer to create routines that showcase their skills. Turntablists often 'battle' against each other in competitions.

Turning the tables

For decades, DJs used only vinyl records. Today, many DJs store their music on CD and mix tracks together using 'CDJs' – CD players that are designed specifically for DJs. Some DJs store their music as MP3 files on laptop computers, mixing it together with software programs. Whatever format the music comes in, and whatever equipment is used, DJing is still about playing music that an audience loves.

DJ masters

The best DJs not only play music, they also make it. They create songs and versions of other people's records, called remixes. The world's best DJs are music producers, too, who find fame playing to huge audiences around the world.

DAVID GUETTA

Just genius

Type 'David Guetta' into www.youtube.com to hear his work.

THE STATS

Name: David Guetta
Born: 7 November 1967
Place of birth: Paris, France
Nationality: French
Job: DJ and producer

David's fifth album featured Snoop Dogg, Lil Wayne, Usher and Jessie J as guest artists.

Party people

Award-winning DJ David Guetta grew up in Paris, France. From an early age he loved to listen to hip-hop on the radio, and discovered house music when a Farley Jackmaster Funk track gripped his imagination. By his early teens, he was making mixtapes and organising parties for his friends in the basement of his parents' house.

Going underground

Before he was 20, David had taken off as a DJ on the underground club scene in Paris. In the late-1980s, his love and knowledge of house music led to a slot on the French music station Radio Nova, and by the mid-1990s he was playing in the capital city's biggest clubs. In 2001, he co-founded his own record label, Gum Productions, and released his first hit single *Just a Little More Love,* featuring Chris Willis. In 2002, David followed the hit with a debut album by the same name.

Guetta blaster

Following his first album, David blasted his way into clubs around the world and into the record collections of millions of people. His next albums, *Guetta Blaster* (2004) and *Pop Life* (2007), sold more than half a million copies. His tracks often feature the biggest names in pop, from Rihanna and Kelly Rowland to Fergie and will.i.am from The Black Eyed Peas.

Career highlights

2001 *Just a Little More Love* was used on the soundtrack to the film *The Football Factory*

2009 released hit *When Love Takes Over*, winning two Grammy Awards

2010 won World Music Award for World's Best DJ

2011 won Grammy Award for Best Remixed Recording for *Revolver* by Madonna, and three International Dance Music Awards including Best Producer

2011 released fifth studio album, *Nothing But the Beat*

Sky's the limit

Today, David is top of the list of producers that people want to work with, and his remixes have been smash hits, selling millions of downloads.

David is also one of the world's best underground-to-mainstream crossover talents. As a master DJ, he can appeal to a pop audience one day and play a club set the same night. With almost as many followers on Facebook as the US president, David is one of the most popular and successful DJs of all time.

To find out more about the female DJ scene, take a look at www.shejay.net

WHERE ARE ALL THE GIRLS?

Flick through DJ and dance-music magazines and you will find some outstanding female DJs. Yet their numbers are few in comparison to the men that dominate the industry. Why are there so few female DJs?

Men at work

Until the early 1990s, there were few female nightclub DJs. Although there were plenty of women in bands, and big dance-music hits often featured female singers, not many women tried DJing.

Here come the girls

By the start of the 1990s, more women were becoming successful in their careers, which encouraged other women to follow their dreams. Women who felt passionately about dance music started to carve out careers in DJing. Female DJs such as DJ Rap, Sister Bliss and Anne Savage made names for themselves on the club scene and proved that women could perform just as well as men.

Time for change

Today, women DJs are making their way in the dance music world. Although their numbers have grown since the early days of DJing, female DJs are still outnumbered by men. The main reason for this is that DJing has been dominated by men for the last 50 years, so as a result many girls have been put off making a career out of DJing. Many people still expect to see a male DJ on the decks, which can be intimidating for women who want to give it a go. 'There are simply more men than women DJing,' says Claudia Cazacu, who was described by DJ Magazine as the number one female DJ on the planet. 'I think if there were more women active on the scene we'd see more women at the very top.'

Sisters are doing it for themselves

Many of the world's top female DJs are trying to get other women interested in DJing. A German techno DJ, producer and record label owner, called Anja Schneider, now runs an annual competition for up-and-coming female DJs called 'Next Girl DJ'. Another group of female DJs set up a website called 'Shejay' to encourage more women to take to the decks. Claudia Cazacu is supportive of their message and says: 'I'm not sure why fewer women choose to follow a career as a DJ because it is honestly the best job I could ever dream of.' So, girls, if you're reading this, come on – hit the decks and give DJing a go!

TURNTABLE GIRL

My story by Sara Simms
(A.K.A. Ychuck)

Type 'DJ Ychuck' into
www.youtube.com to
see Sara turntabling.

I first fell in love with music when I was 14 years old and my mum took me to a music shop to buy my first vinyl record. By the time I was 17, I'd decided I wanted to be a DJ. I used to spend all my time at the weekends going to big parties in Toronto, Canada. And when I saw great DJs playing, I couldn't wait to buy my first pair of turntables and a mixer and give it a go myself.

I found out about turntablism and the DJ battle scene when my friend, DJ Fathom, suggested that I watch a video of an International Turntable Federation (ITF) DJ competition. This is a competition in which DJs battle for the prize of best turntablist. The video was amazing – I was mesmerised! From that day onwards, I knew I wanted to be a turntablist.

My first-ever DJ gig was at a late-night party in Toronto. I performed my first turntablism set with some hip-hop records and included scratches and beat juggles. I was so nervous that I wrote down my routine on a sheet of paper so that I could look at it during my set!

Since then, I've not looked back. I'm really lucky that I am asked to play all over the world. Last week I played at a party on the beach in Cannes, France. I've also played at DJ battles in the USA, hip-hop festivals in Berlin and lots of parties in Canada. One amazing opportunity I had was when DJ Qbert, one of the greatest living turntablists, invited me to star in a tutorial video featured on his Skratch University website.

I love being a turntablist and wouldn't do anything else. Through playing music and performing to hundreds and thousands of people, I get to do what I love – for a living! It makes me so happy when I put on a great show that the crowd enjoy – it's the best feeling in the world!

THE CHEMICAL BROTHERS

THE STATS

Name: Tom Rowlands and Ed Simons
Born: 11 January 1971 (Tom); 9 June 1970 (Ed)
Place of birth: London
Nationality: British
Job: DJs, producers and musicians

Student dreams

Tom Rowlands and Ed Simons first started DJing together as university students in Manchester, England, where they shared a house. First as The 237 Turbo Nutters and later as The Dust Brothers, they played a mix of hip-hop, house and techno music in clubs around the city. In 1991, they decided to make their own music to play in their sets, and in 1992 recorded *Song to the Siren*. The record was then signed to the Junior Boys Own label by Andrew Weatherall, the most popular DJ/producer of the time.

Electronic masters

Thanks to a trademark sound that appeals to rock fans as much as hip-hop lovers and dance music enthusiasts, The Chemical Brothers have become one of the best-known electronic bands. To date, the band has released seven albums, toured worldwide countless times and played live shows at some of the world's biggest music festivals. In 2011, Tom and Ed were invited to compose the soundtrack to the film *Hanna* – something that only three other DJs (Orbital, Daft Punk and David Holmes) had ever done before.

Big beat pioneers

After leaving university in 1993, The Dust Brothers released a record called *Chemical Beats*. Combining hip-hop, house and techno, it was a huge club hit and inspired a new wave of 'big beat' producers such as Fatboy Slim. Following this success, Tom and Ed began to DJ around the UK and in 1995, they were asked to produce their debut album, *Exit Planet Dust*, as The Chemical Brothers. They were soon DJing worldwide and by the end of the 1990s, The Chemical Brothers were one of the biggest electronic music acts in the world.

Type 'Chemical Brothers Galvanise' into www.youtube.com to hear one of their most famous tracks.

15

TOM THORPE

Club DJ Tom Thorpe has been DJing since he was 17. He regularly plays throughout Europe and Australia. He also founded the Asylum club night in Leeds, UK, and is one half of production duo PBR Streetgang. Radar spoke to Tom to find out more about the world of a DJ…

What attracted you to the idea of being a DJ?

I went to my first underground club when I was 17, and it blew me away. The DJs seemed to rule the night – I was hooked there and then.

When did you first give DJing a try?

I was 16 years old when I first played on a pair of decks. I can remember it being really difficult. I really wanted to be good, so I kept on practising.

What's your favourite music to play to a crowd?

It depends on the crowd, the party and the size of the room. If I'm in front of a large crowd in a big room, then I play house music. For a small, intimate venue, I tend to play music that is 'disco' in sound.

What's the best way to learn DJ skills?

There is only one way to perfect your DJ skills… practise! The more basic the equipment you start on, the more you will understand how to play properly. It's so much harder playing on poor-quality equipment (especially turntables).

What makes a good DJ stand out from the rest?

A good DJ will show their passion and flair not only through their music, but also with their body language when they play. If you are 100 per cent into it, it shows.

What's the best way to build up your music collection?

A physical format – vinyl or CD – is best. I spend the most money on vinyl, and it is still my preferred format. I sometimes buy a track on vinyl *and* download – I archive the vinyl and play the download.

Who are your favourite DJs right now?

Where do I start?! I like Laurent Garnier, Maurice Fulton, Felix da Housecat, Lindstrøm, Deadmau5, Theo Parrish, Crazy P, DJ Harvey, Greg Wilson, The Unabombers, The Bays, Kenny Dope, Louie Vega, Kerri Chandeller, Daniele Baldelli – all great DJs still active on the club scene today.

TURNING TABLES

Every year, the world's top turntablists play at the Disco Mix Club (DMC) in a competition called the DMC World DJ Championships. There are thousands of turntablists around the world, but here are some of the best.

1. Grandmaster Flash

In the 1970s, in New York City, USA, Grandmaster Flash was the first DJ to perfect the art of scratching. He was just a teenager at the time. The pioneering DJ later created what became known as 'beat juggling' and built the first-ever DJ mixer with a cross-fader, which allowed him to quickly switch between records playing on two different turntables. In 1981, he released the first-ever record created using three turntables, a mixer and a pile of records: *The Adventures of Grandmaster Flash on the Wheels of Steel*.

2. DJ Rafik

German turntablist DJ Rafik grew up playing the drums before taking up DJing at the age of 13. By 25, he had won a record six DMC World DJ Championship titles. He is now one of the world's most in-demand DJs and regularly experiments with new DJ techniques and equipment.

3. The Scratch Perverts

The Scratch Perverts are the world's most famous turntablist team. The four-man team takes part in competitions such as the DMC World DJ Championships, playing impressive routines using eight turntables and four mixers connected together. The Scratch Perverts are famous for scratching and beat juggling over different musical styles such as hip-hop, drum and bass, dubstep and reggae.

4. DJ A-Trak

In 1997, DJ A-Trak shocked the turntablist community by becoming the youngest ever winner of the DMC World DJ Championships. The Canadian was just 15 years old when he took the title, proving that if you are good enough to DJ, you are old enough!

5. DJ Cash Money

Widely regarded as the finest turntablist of all time, DJ Cash Money was the first DJ to be included in the Technics DJ Hall Of Fame. After finding success in his home city of Philadelphia, USA, in the mid-1980s, he became a worldwide star. In 1988, he won the DMC World DJ Championships.

Type 'turntable tutorial 1' into www.youtube.com to find out how to start turntabling.

RISE OF THE DJ

Throughout history, people have always danced to music. The discotheques in France in the 1940s gave British dancehall owner Jimmy Savile the idea to become the world's first 'disc jockey'. In 1947, he experimented with two turntables, and the idea quickly caught on.

The Jamaican-born DJ, Kool Herc is one of the pioneers of house music.

The first mixers

During the 1950s and 1960s, people gathered at 'record hops' to dance to the latest pop music played by a local DJ. But it was in New York City, USA, in the 1970s that the idea of a DJ as a performer took off. A DJ called Francis Grasso became the first man to mix records together at a nightclub. Soon dancers were flocking to clubs to hear DJs such as Larry Levan and Walter Gibbons.

Keep on moving

It was in the Bronx, New York City, in the 1970s that the first turntablists developed. At illegal street gatherings called 'block parties', DJs such as Kool Herc and Grandmaster Flash helped develop the style that would become known as hip-hop. They also invented scratching and beat juggling to help them to stand out from rival DJs, marking the beginning of turntablism.

Making music

In 1985, DJs in Chicago, USA, such as Farley Jackmaster Funk, Ron Hardy and Frankie Knuckles began to use drum machines and samplers to make their own music. Inspired by disco, they created house music – so called because it was played at a nightclub called The Warehouse. Since then, DJs have helped develop many new styles of music, from drum and bass to garage and dubstep.

> Type 'DJ Kool Herc' into www.youtube.com to find out more.

Superstar DJs

The internet has allowed performances to be heard worldwide and DJs do not just play at clubs anymore. Music festivals from Brazil to Barcelona bring clubbers together from around the world. The Winter Music Conference in Miami, USA, and the summer months on the Mediterranean island of Ibiza are also important dates in the diary of a DJ or clubber.

British superstar DJ Pete Tong has been a huge influence on DJs around the world. His radio shows are broadcast worldwide via the internet.

Glowsticks, bells and whistles

The biggest change to DJing in the last 20 years has come through the development of new technology. CD turntables, DJ mixers with built-in special effects, and computer DJing software have all helped revolutionise the way people play music in nightclubs. Now DJs have the tools to make their sets exciting and original – the only limit is their imagination!

FELIX DA HOUSECAT

One cool cat

Funky Felix

As a child, Felix Stallings Jr was into funk and soul, which his father played on the saxophone. However, Felix soon fine-tuned his own tastes, becoming a huge fan of Chicago house, and a massive admirer of the rock idol Prince. By the age of 14, Felix was making house music at home on his four-track recording equipment.

Study leave

Aged just 15, Felix got his first break when he met a pioneer of acid house, DJ Pierre, who helped him make his first single, *Phantasy Girl*. Felix's parents had other plans for their son, however. They encouraged him to enrol at Alabama State University and leave his turntables and house music behind.

Who's that cat?

Felix's girlfriend was into house music, and as a result Felix began mixing and producing when he left university. DJ Pierre helped him release the record *Thee Dawn* in 1992, which gave him his big break in Europe. Felix then formed Radikal Fear Records – one of the top house labels in the world in the 1990s. He released more of his own hits, and those by artists such as DJ Sneak and Armando. People know Felix as Felix da Housecat, but he has also recorded under many names including Aphrohead, Thee Maddkatt Courtship and Sharkimaxx. He has also released seven mix compilation albums.

Alias Felix

Felix's music can be heard on the soundtracks to video games, TV shows and movies. He has remixed tracks for P Diddy (*Jack U*), Madonna (*American Life*), Kylie (*Where is the Feeling?*), and Britney Spears (*Toxic*). It is hard to keep up with just how many amazing tunes he is responsible for (his aliases make it tricky!), but industry insiders agree that the funky feline has created some of dance music's greatest-ever tracks.

In his mid-30s, Felix already has a long and successful career behind him.

THE STATS

Name: Felix da Housecat (Felix Stallings Jr)
Born: 25 August 1971
Place of birth: Chicago, USA
Nationality: American
Job: Producer and DJ

Career highlights

1995 released his first full-length album, *Alone in the Dark*

2001 won Best Album for *Kittenz and Thee Glitz* at the Muzik Awards, beating electro-stalwarts Daft Punk

2003 nominated for Grammy Award for remix of *Lost Love*

2011 released the album, *Son of Analogue*, for free on the cover of *Mixmag* magazine

BEAT SPEAK

Sometimes, DJs seem to have a language all of their own…

acid house
a variant of Chicago house music with a repetitive and hypnotic style

battle records
tracks with good beats and samples for scratching and juggling

beat juggling
using a cross-fader to quickly flick between two copies of the same track

beat match
also called beat mix – to blend two tracks of the same speed together so that the drum rhythms are seamless and the beats 'match'

cue up
to line up a track in the place where you want it to start playing

decks
a set of turntables

drum machine
an electronic instrument that makes the sound of drums and can be programmed to play set sequences

dub mix
a version of a track that has been stripped back to its basic parts

four-track
a piece of equipment for recording and mixing together four separate instruments

juggling
working with two samples on more than one mixer or turntable

MC
someone who jive-rhymes or raps over the top of tracks

mix
tracks that run together one after another, without a break

phasing
playing two copies of the same track together, but slightly out of time, for creative effect

promo
a promotional copy of a track sent out by a record label to advertise an artist or song

raves
huge dance parties, often held outdoors or in disused buildings instead of in established nightclubs

residency
when a DJ is permanently based at a specific club

sampling
taking a section of a track and reusing it somewhere else

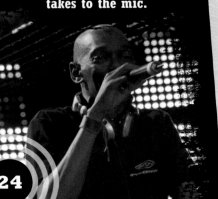

MC for dance act Faithless, Maxi Jazz, takes to the mic.

scratching
twisting a track backwards and forwards whilst altering the cross-fader

signature tune
a track that a DJ becomes famous for playing

sound system
the equipment needed to play music at a volume and quality that fills a room

set
a performance by a DJ that is made up of tracks chosen because of the way they work together

slip-cue
starting a track on its first beat by holding it still while the turntable spins without it

white label
a promotional copy of a track given to DJs ahead of the track's official release

GLOSSARY

Scratching is most commonly associated with hip-hop music.

adrenalin
a hormone found in the human body that causes the heart to beat faster

amps
short for amplifiers – the electrical equipment that makes music loud enough to play out through speakers

channels
the name given to the inputs on a mixer into which sound sources (for example, vinyl or CD turntables) are plugged

cross-fader
a control feature on a mixer used to blend the sounds coming out of two or more channels

euphoric
feeling extremely happy

fader
a sliding control used to alter the sound levels of a channel

label
a company in charge of making and releasing a record

mainstream
popular with a large proportion of the public

mixer
a piece of equipment used by DJs to mix sounds from a number of different sources

pioneer
one of the first people to do or be involved in something

pitch-control function
a feature on vinyl and CD turntables that allows DJs to speed up or slow down music

pop music
short for popular music, widely played on radio and TV

producer
a person in charge of mixing and arranging the music to make a record

record
any form of recorded music

turntable
a device used to play vinyl records

underground
hidden or secret; not well known to many people

vinyl
a type of pressed plastic traditionally used to make records

HIT RECORDS

3

The age that the toddler who would become DJ Jack started playing his dad's records. At six, he played his first gig and today holds three world records for being the youngest DJ in the world.

10,000

The average number of clubbers who dance the night away at the world's biggest dance club, Privilege, in Ibiza, Spain.

4

The number of decks US house DJ Donald Glaude uses to mix his sets.

250,000

The number of revellers who flocked to Fatboy Slim's Big Beach

1,400+

The number of DJs and artists at the world-famous Winter Music Conference in Miami, USA, in 2011.

10

The average number of hours in DJ/Producer Danny Tenaglia's sets. He regularly plays from midnight until 10am the next day!

27

… gigs in 25 days. That is DJ Tiësto's record. In 2010, he performed an exhausting 21 consecutive gigs in 21 days.

£300,000

The amount of money top club DJs can make in just one year.

50,000

The estimated number of records owned by club and radio DJ, Gilles Peterson.

Professional DJs are techno wizards who use a range of equipment to play a set.

On the decks

Also known as turntables, decks have traditionally been used by DJs to play vinyl records. Decks designed for DJ use include a pitch-control function, which allows the DJ to speed up or slow down a record in order to get it in time when mixing between songs.

Mixing it up

The mixer is a DJ's most important piece of equipment. It allows him or her to move between two or more sound sources and present a seamless mix of music. Each sound source (for example, two different turntables or two CD players and a microphone) is plugged into a different 'channel' on the mixer.

Fading across

Most mixers have a cross-fader, used by the DJ to switch between different channels. Pushing the cross-fader from one side to the other is known as mixing. The cross-fader also plays a vital role in tricks such as scratching and beat juggling.

mixer

vinyl decks

CD turntable

Technology tunes

Many DJs now use computer software or digital control systems to play their sets. Software programs such as PCDJ, MixMeister and Ableton Live let DJs mix between songs stored on a laptop computer as MP3 files. With digital control systems such as Serato Scratch Live, Torque and Traktor Pro, DJs mix songs stored on their laptops using special 'control records' on regular turntables. Digital control systems are very popular with turntablists.

Head start

Headphones allow a DJ to hear a record before it is played over the sound system. This lets the DJ listen to each track independently, match the beats and cue it up. Being able to listen to a track before it is mixed in is very important to DJs, because it helps them to monitor sound levels and check whether the song is perfectly in time with what is already playing over the sound system.

MUSICIANS OR JUKEBOXES?

FOR

Many people believe that DJing is an artform in its own right and as a result DJs should be treated as musicians. They argue that:

1. The best DJs have a wide musical knowledge and an intuitive understanding of what makes people dance. They use these skills to take their audiences on a journey through different styles, sounds and rhythms.
2. Like other musicians, many DJs use their creativity and skill to give their audience an enthralling live performance.
3. Turntablists have proved that two turntables, a mixer and a pile of records can be used as an instrument. Creative turntablists are always looking for ways to create new sounds and musical effects using simple equipment.
4. DJing has changed the way people make music. It was DJs who first used loops and samples as the basis of records – now bands, singers and producers routinely use samples in their music.

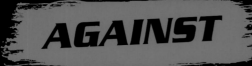

AGAINST

Other people believe that DJing is nothing more than putting tracks on a machine and that DJs should not be regarded as artists. They argue that:

1. All that is required to DJ is a basic grasp of mixing music, something that can be learnt in the space of a few days.
2. Most DJs are nothing more than glorified 'jukeboxes'. All they do is play recorded music.
3. DJs who play music made by other people are not doing anything creative, they are making money from the hard work of real musicians, singers and songwriters.
4. The success of the music video game *DJ Hero* proves that DJing is little more than matching beats. Music made by DJs is simple, repetitive and formulaic. It is of less musical value or worth than songs written by musicians.

RIGHT OR WRONG?

DJing can be a great platform for musical creativity and inventiveness, offering people the opportunity to take music in new directions. However, DJs can be considered artists only if they actually create something new rather than just play other people's music. A lazy DJ is a bad DJ!

HERE YOU GO!

If scratching, mixing and looping is on your playlist, check out Radar's guide.

Talk to the pros

There are lots of DJs online who can help you get your set style up to speed:
www.learn2dj.co.uk

Spread the word

Upload your mixes, get feedback and promote your DJ skills:
www.soundcloud.com
www.mixcloud.com

Pay to play

Really committed? Try a DJ course:
www.ministryofsound.com/club/dj-academy

Reads & Apps

How to DJ (Properly) by Frank Broughton and Bill Brewster (Bantam Press, 2002)

Master This! DJing by Matt Anniss (Wayland, 2009)

Take a look at the best DJ and music magazines:
www.mixmag.net
www.djmag.com

Want to know what that song is? *Shazam* is a free app that can tell you:
www.shazam.com

Turn your phone into a mini DJ booth with *Cue Play DJ* and *Touch DJ*!
www.itunes.com
http://amidio.com
https://market.android.com

INDEX